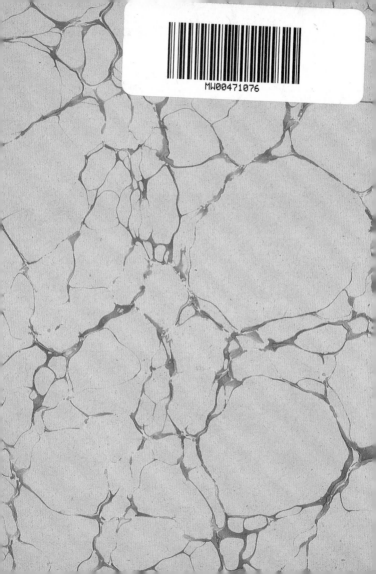

MW00471076

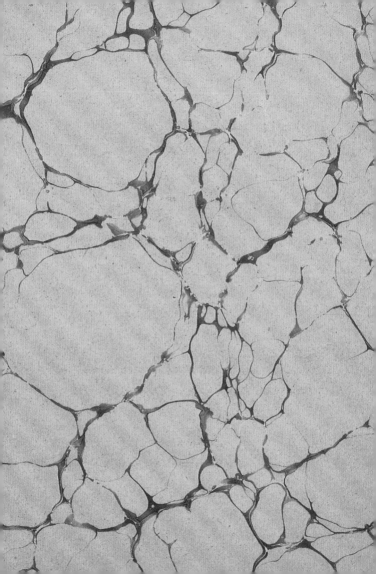

Memento

Solace for Grieving

Give sorrow words; the grief that does not speak
Whispers the o'er-fraught heart, and bids it break.

SHAKESPEARE, from *Macbeth,* act 4, scene 3

Memento

Solace for Grieving

Edited and compiled by
MICHELE DURKSON CLISE

A BULFINCH PRESS BOOK
LITTLE, BROWN AND COMPANY

BOSTON · NEW YORK · TORONTO · LONDON

Once you shone among the living as the
    Morning Star;
Among the dead you shine now, as the
    Evening Star.

PLATO

IN COLLECTING SAYINGS AND POEMS for various projects, I have come across evocative bits of poetry and prose that celebrate life while expressing the poignancy of its loss. Words are only words, but if taken as messengers of the heart to be examined and relied upon in moments of private reflection, they can comfort us in times of seemingly never-ending grief. To be able to offer consolation to a grieving friend is one of life's most tender acts.

These small, yet complete, tributes are comforting in their affirmation of the endless cycles of love and life. As a dear friend in the theater once said, "life is not a rehearsal." Rather, it is a gift to be enjoyed and shared, so let us find pleasure in what we have and have had. In the face of death, we must savor the essence of the person we loved, not the loss of their company.

My hope here is that, with the addition of a photo or a few personal words, this small book might become a repository for the heart's emotions in a time of mourning. In remembering, there is solace; in sharing, there is consolation.

MICHELE DURKSON CLISE

When I am dead, my dearest,
    Sing no sad songs for me;
Plant thou no roses at my head,
    Nor shady cypress tree:
Be the green grass above me
    With showers and dewdrops wet;
And if thou wilt, remember,
    And if thou wilt, forget.

I shall not see the shadows,
    I shall not feel the rain;
I shall not hear the nightingale
    Sing on, as if in pain:
And dreaming through the twilight
    That doth not rise nor set,
Haply I may remember,
    And haply may forget.

CHRISTINA ROSSETTI, "Song"

Silence is no certain token
That no secret grief is there;
Sorrow which is never spoken
Is the heaviest load to bear.

FRANCES RIDLEY HAVERGAL, "Misunderstood," stanza 15

There are times when sorrow seems to be the only truth.

OSCAR WILDE, from *De Profundis*

Stop all the clocks, cut off the telephone,
Prevent the dog from barking with a juicy bone,
Silence the pianos and with muffled drum
Bring out the coffin, let the mourners come.

Let aeroplanes circle moaning overhead
Scribbling on the sky the message He Is Dead,
Put crêpe bows round the white necks of the public
    doves,
Let the traffic policemen wear black cotton gloves.

He was my North, my South, my East and West,
My working week and my Sunday rest,
My noon, my midnight, my talk, my song;
I thought that love would last for ever: I was wrong.

The stars are not wanted now: put out every one;
Pack up the moon and dismantle the sun:
Pour away the ocean and sweep up the wood;
For nothing now can ever come to any good.

W. H. AUDEN, from "Funeral Blues"

We thought the years would last forever,
They are all gone now, the days
We thought would not come for us are here.
Bright trout poised in the current —
The raccoon's track at the water's edge —
A bittern booming in the distance —
Your ashes scattered on this mountain —
Moving seaward on this stream.

KENNETH REXROTH, from "Andree Rexroth"

Never more will the wind
Cherish you again,
Never more will the rain.

Never more
Shall we find you bright
In the snow and wind.

The snow is melted,
The snow is gone,
And you are flown:

Like a bird out of our hand,
Like a light out of our heart,
You are gone.

HILDA DOOLITTLE, from "Hymen"

Grief fills the room up of my absent child,
Lies in his bed, walks up and down with me,
Puts on his pretty looks, repeats his words,
Remembers me of all his gracious parts,
Stuffs out his vacant garments with his form:
Then have I reason to be fond of grief.

SHAKESPEARE, from *King John*, act 3, scene 4

She's dead – but in my grief
I forget,
and as though she were still alive,
I keep asking,
"Where's she gotten to!"

In this world
there are many kinds of longing,
but no longing to match
the longing for one's child

KI NO TSURAYUKI, "On a dead child, from the *Tosa Diary*"

I loved my friend.
He went away from me.
There's nothing more to say,
The poem ends,
Soft as it began —
I loved my friend.

LANGSTON HUGHES, "Poem"

The sound of her silk skirt has stopped.
On the marble pavement dust grows.
Her empty room is cold and still.
Fallen leaves are piled against the doors.
  Longing for that lovely lady.
How can I bring my aching heart to rest?

WU TI

This world of dew
is only a world of dew—
and yet

ISSA

Musa the blue-eyed, the sweetly singing nightingale,
Lies here suddenly mute in this little grave,
Still as a stone, who was once so witty, so much loved:

Pretty Musa, may this dust rest lightly upon you.

ANONYMOUS, "Epitaph of the Singing-Girl Musa"

I am not resigned to the shutting away of loving
    hearts in the hard ground.
So it is, and so it will be, for so it has been, time out of
    mind:
Into the darkness they go, the wise and the lovely.
    Crowned
With lilies and with laurel they go; but I am not
    resigned.

Lovers and thinkers, into the earth with you.
Be one with the dull, the indiscriminate dust.
A fragment of what you felt, of what you knew,
A formula, a phrase remains, — but the best is lost.

The answers quick and keen, the honest look, the
    laughter, the love, —
They are gone. They have gone to feed the roses.
    Elegant and curled
Is the blossom. Fragrant is the blossom. I know. But I
    do not approve.
More precious was the light in your eyes than all the
    roses in the world.

Down, down, down into the darkness of the grave
Gently they go, the beautiful, the tender, the kind;
Quietly they go, the intelligent, the witty, the brave.
I know. But I do not approve. And I am not resigned.

EDNA ST. VINCENT MILLAY, "Dirge Without Music"

So fades a summer cloud away;
  So sinks the gale when storms are o'er;
So gently shuts the eye of day;
  So dies a wave along the shore.

ANNA LETITIA BARBAULD, from *The Death of the Virtuous*

The Bustle in a House
The Morning after Death
Is solemnest of industries
Enacted upon Earth —

The Sweeping up the Heart
And putting Love away
We shall not want to use again
Until Eternity.

EMILY DICKINSON, "The Bustle in a House"

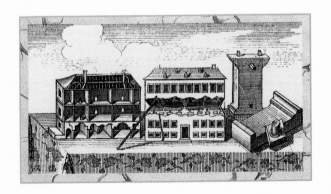

Oh death
about you I know nothing, nothing –
about the afterwards
as a matter of fact we know nothing.

Yet oh death, oh death
also I know so much about you
the knowledge is within me, without being a matter of
    fact.

And so I know
after the painful, painful experience of dying
there comes an after-gladness, a strange joy
in a great adventure
oh the great adventure of death, where Thomas Cook
    cannot guide us.

I have always wanted to be as flowers are
so unhampered in their living and dying,
and in death I believe I shall be as the flowers are.

I shall blossom like a dark pansy, and be delighted
there among the dark sun-rays of death.
I can feel myself unfolding in the dark sunshine of
    death
to something flowery and fulfilled, and with a strange
    sweet perfume.

D. H. LAWRENCE, "Gladness of Death"

Here are cakes for thy body,
Cool water for thy throat,
Sweet breezes for thy nostrils,
And thou art satisfied.

No longer dost thou stumble
Upon thy chosen path,
From thy mind all evil
And darkness fall away.

Here by the river,
Drink and bathe thy limbs,
Or cast thy net, and surely
It shall be filled with fish.

The holy cow of Hapi
Shall give thee of her milk,
The ale of gods triumphant
Shall be thy daily draught.

White linen is thy tunic,
Thy sandals shine with gold;
Victorious thy weapons,
That death come not again.

Now upon the whirlwind
Thou followest thy Prince,
Now thou hast refreshment
Under the leafy tree.

Take wings to climb the zenith,
Or sleep in Fields of Peace;
By day the Sun shall keep thee,
By night the rising Star.

from *The Egyptian Book of the Dead*

Suns may set and rise; we, when our short day has closed, must sleep on during one never-ending night.

CATULLUS, from *Carmina*, act 5, scene 4

Warm summer sun shine kindly here:
Warm summer wind blow softly here:
Green sod above lie light, lie light:
Good-night, Dear Heart: good-night, good-night.

memorial to Clorinda Haywood, St. Bartholomew's, Edgbaston, England

At the first strokes of the fiddle bow
the dancers rise from their seats.
The dance begins to shape itself
in the crowd, as couples join,
and couples join couples, their movement
together lightening their feet.
They move in the ancient circle
of the dance. The dance and the song
call each other into being. Soon
they are one — rapt in a single
rapture, so that even the night
has its clarity, and time
is the wheel that brings it round.
In this rapture the dead return.
Sorrow is gone from them.
They are light. They step
into the steps of the living
and turn with them in the dance
in the sweet enclosure
of the song, and timeless
is the wheel that brings it round

WENDELL BERRY, "The Wheel"

Never the spirit was born; the spirit
    shall cease to be never;
Never was time it was not; End and
    Beginning are dreams!
Birthless and deathless and changeless
    remaineth the spirit for ever;
Death hath not touched it at all, dead
    though the house of it seems.

from *The Bhagavad-Gita*

And who shall separate the dust
Which later we shall be:
Whose keen discerning eye will scan
And solve the mystery?

The high, the low, the rich, the poor,
The black, the white, the red,
And all the chromatique between,
Of whom shall it be said:

Here lies the dust of Africa;
Here are the sons of Rome;
Here lies one unlabelled
The world at large his home!

Can one then separate the dust,
Will mankind lie apart,
When life has settled back again
The same as from the start?

GEORGIA DOUGLAS JOHNSON, "Common Dust"

In a dream I meet
my dead friend. He has,
I know, gone long and far,
and yet he is the same
for the dead are changeless.
They grow no older.
It is I who have changed,
grown strange to what I was.
Yet I, the changed one,
ask: "How you been?"
He grins and looks at me.
"I been eating peaches
off some mighty fine trees."

WENDELL BERRY, "A Meeting"

Sorrow, lie still and wear
No tears, no sighings, no despair,
  No mourning weeds,
  Nought that discloses
  A heart that bleeds;
But looks contented I will bear,
  And o'er my cheeks strew roses.
Unto the world I may not weep,
But save my sorrow all, and keep
  A secret heart, sweet soul, for thee,
  As the great earth and swelling sea —

THOMAS LOVELL BEDDOES, "Dirge"

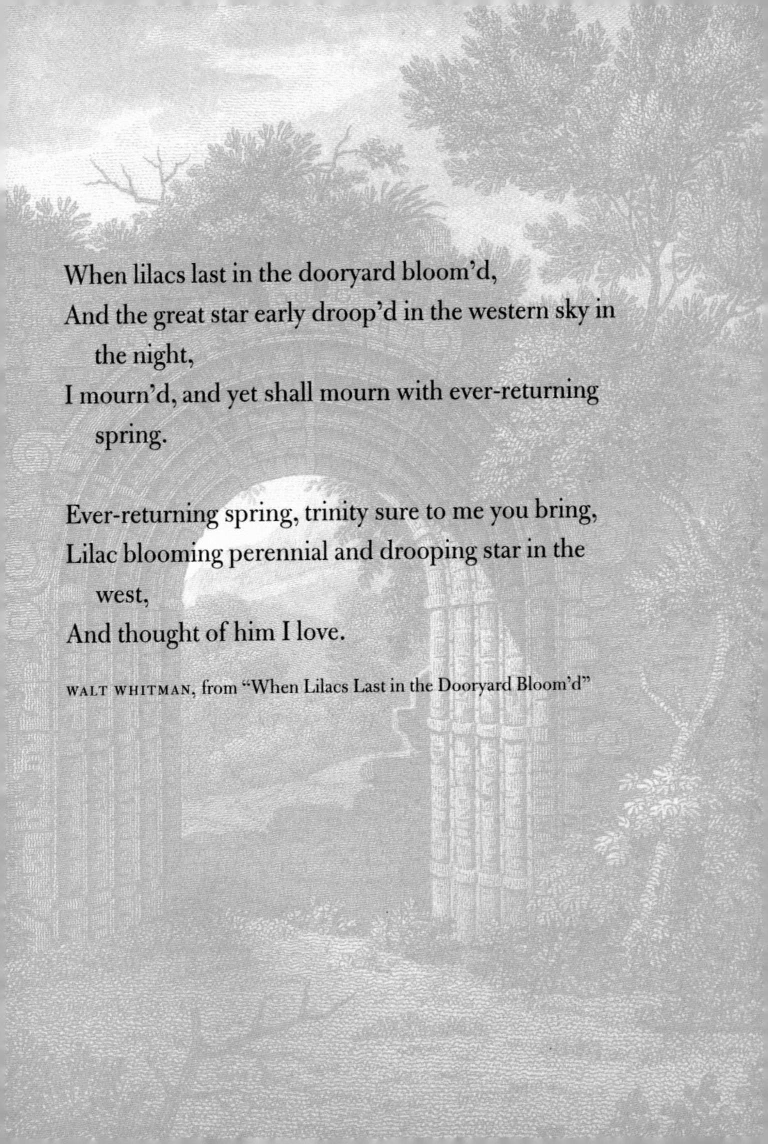

When lilacs last in the dooryard bloom'd,
And the great star early droop'd in the western sky in
the night,
I mourn'd, and yet shall mourn with ever-returning
spring.

Ever-returning spring, trinity sure to me you bring,
Lilac blooming perennial and drooping star in the
west,
And thought of him I love.

WALT WHITMAN, from "When Lilacs Last in the Dooryard Bloom'd"

Our revels now are ended. These our actors,
As I foretold you, were all spirits, and
Are melted into air, into thin air;
And, like the baseless fabric of this vision,
The cloud-capped towers, the gorgeous palaces,
The solemn temples, the great globe itself,
Yes, all which it inherit, shall dissolve,
And, like this insubstantial pageant faded,
Leave not a rack behind. We are such stuff
As dreams are made on, and our little life
Is rounded with a sleep.

SHAKESPEARE, from *The Tempest,* act 4, scene 1

All the flowers of the spring
Meet to perfume our burying;
These have but their growing prime,
And man does flourish but his time:
Survey our progress from our birth;
We are set, we grow, we turn to earth.
Courts adieu, and all delights,
All bewitching appetites!
Sweetest breath and clearest eye,
Like perfumes, go out and die;
And consequently this is done
As shadows wait upon the sun.
Vain the ambition of kings
Who seek by trophies and dead things
To leave a living name behind,
And weave but nets to catch the wind.

JOHN WEBSTER, from *The Devil's Law Case*

Those who are dead are never gone:
They are there in the thickening shadow.
The dead are not under the earth:
they are in the tree that rustles,
they are in the wood that groans,
they are in the water that sleeps,
they are in the hut, they are in the crowd,
the dead are not dead.

Those who are dead are never gone,
they are in the breast of the woman,
they are in the child who is wailing
and in the firebrand that flames.
The dead are not under the earth:
they are in the fire that is dying,
they are in the grasses that weep,
they are in the whimpering rocks,
they are in the forest, they are in the house,
the dead are not dead.

BIRAGO DIOP

One brought me the news of your death, O
    Herakleitos my friend,
And I wept for you, remembering
How often we had watched the sun set as we talked.

And you are ashes now, old friend from
    Halikarnassos,
Ashes now:
           but your nightingale songs live on,
And Death, the destroyer of every lovely thing,
Shall not touch them with his blind all-canceling
    fingers.

KALLIMACHOS, "Elegy on Herakleitos"

When he shall die,
Take him and cut him out in little stars,
And he will make the face of heaven so fine
That all the world will be in love with night,
And pay no worship to the garish sun.

SHAKESPEARE, from *Romeo and Juliet,* act 3, scene 2

In the day of his work
when the grace of the world
was upon him, he made his way,
not turning back or looking aside,
light in his stride.

Now may the grace of death
be upon him, his spirit blessed
in deep song of the world
and the stars turning, the seasons
returning, and long rest.

WENDELL BERRY, from "Requiem"

Let us turn over the page
And see what is written
On the other side of the night.

THOMAS MC GRATH, from "Graveyard Shift"

The wings of man's life are plumed with the feathers
   of death.

from a petition addressed to Queen Elizabeth by a seaman

Acknowledgments

The editor is grateful to the following publishers and copyright holders for permission to use selections reprinted in this book:

Excerpt from "Funeral Blues" from *W. H. Auden: Collected Poems* by W. H. Auden, edited by Edward Mendelson. Copyright © 1940 and renewed 1968 by W. H. Auden. Reprinted in the U.S., Canada, and the Open Market by permission of Random House, Inc., and in the British Commonwealth (excluding Canada) by Faber and Faber Ltd., London.

"A Meeting," excerpt from "Requiem," and "The Wheel," from *Collected Poems 1957–1982* by Wendell Berry. Copyright © 1984 by Wendell Berry. Reprinted by permission of North Point Press, a division of Farrar, Straus & Giroux, Inc.

Untitled poem by Birago Diop from *Jambalaya: The Natural Woman's Book of Personal Charms and Practical Rituals* by Luisah Teish. Copyright © 1985 by Luisah Teish. Reprinted by permission of HarperCollins Publishers, Inc.

Excerpt from "Hymen," from *Collected Poems, 1912–1944.* Copyright © 1982 by The Estate of Hilda Doolittle. Reprinted by permission of New Directions Publishing Corp. and Carcanet Press Limited.

"Epitaph of the Singing-Girl Musa" and "Elegy on Herakleitos" from *Poems from the Greek Anthology* by Dudley Fitts, trans. Copyright © 1956 by New Directions Publishing Corp. Reprinted by permission of New Directions Publishing Corp.

Excerpt from *Sound of Water: Haiku by Bashō, Buson, Issa, and Other Poets,* Sam Hamill, trans. Copyright © 1995. Reprinted by arrangement with Shambhala Publications, Inc., 300 Massachusetts Ave., Boston MA 02115.

"Poem," from *The Dream Keeper and Other Poems* by Langston Hughes. Copyright © 1932 by Alfred A. Knopf, Inc. and renewed 1960 by Langston Hughes. Reprinted by permission of the publisher.

Excerpt from "Graveyard Shift," from *Death Song* by Thomas McGrath. Copyright © 1991 by Thomas McGrath. Reprinted by permission of Copper Canyon Press.

"Dirge Without Music" by Edna St. Vincent Millay, from *Collected Poems,* HarperCollins. Copyright © 1928, 1955 by Edna St. Vincent Millay and Norma Millay Ellis. Reprinted by permission of Elizabeth Barnett, literary executor.

Excerpt from "Andree Rexroth," from *Collected Shorter Poems* by Kenneth Rexroth. Copyright © 1944 by New Directions Publishing Corp. Reprinted by permission of New Directions Publishing Corp.

"On a dead child, from the *Tosa Diary*," from *From the Country of Eight Islands* by Hiroaki Sato and Burton Watson. Copyright © 1981 by Hiroaki Sato and Burton Watson. Reprinted by permission of Doubleday, a division of Bantam Doubleday Dell Publishing Group, Inc.

"Li Fu-jen" by Wu Ti, from *Translations from the Chinese* by Arthur Waley, trans. Copyright © 1919 and renewed 1947 by Arthur Waley. Reprinted by permission of Alfred A. Knopf, Inc.

First Edition

Produced for Bulfinch Press by Marquand Books, Inc.,

Library of Congress Catalog Card Number 95-76697

ISBN 0-8212-2222-8

Bulfinch Press is an imprint and trademark of
Little, Brown and Company (Inc.)

Published simultaneously in Canada by
Little, Brown & Company (Canada) Limited

PRINTED IN HONG KONG

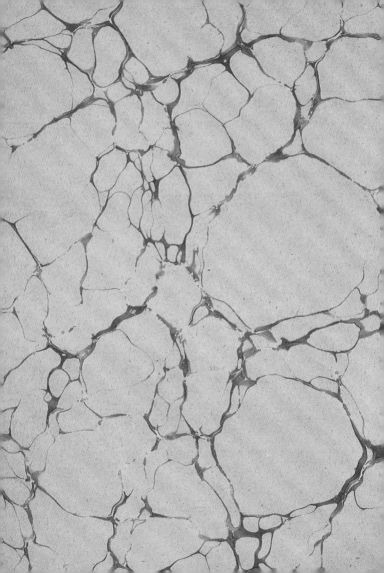

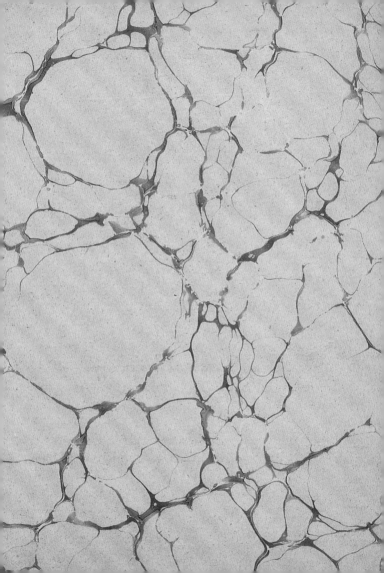